GROWN-UP STUFF EXPLAINED

EXPLAINED

75 Topics 18-Year-Olds Should Know

Witty Ryter

This Page Intentionally Left Blank

To my family. Thanks for listening to my ideas.

Contents

Contents

Contents

Introduction

Hello! You are an adult now. Congratulations and welcome to the big leagues! I wrote this book with the hope of making your transition into adulthood a little easier.

Being a grown-up is definitely more complicated than being a child, but anyone with the proper mindset can handle it. The key is to keep striving to own every role you play after turning 18. The faster you decide that you are in charge of your life and act like it, the better off you'll be.

Before you get too far into this book, I want to clarify that it doesn't tell you how to act like an adult. There are mountains of literature on the subject, so adding to the pile did not make sense to me. Instead, I have built on the fact that most young people take a while to figure things out because they simply don't know what they don't know.

This book aims to help with the knowledge gap by providing you with a list of topics to explore. The material has been greatly simplified for easier consumption, but it should give you a good starting point. My goal is merely to give you a taste of what's out there. It will be up to you to determine what's useful and how much more you want to learn about each topic.

You'll notice that many items relate to money. The reason is that money affects practically all aspects of adult life, directly or indirectly.

I wish that I could give you all the answers, but one of the challenges of being a grown-up is the fact that we are all learning as we go along.

Civic Stuff

US Selective Service System

When is this relevant? When you are an 18-year-old male.

What is it? Every male citizen and lawful immigrant living in the United States must register with the US Selective Service System soon after his 18th birthday.

Registration provides the federal government with a list of people who could join the military in the event of a national emergency.

Why does this matter? Failure to register may result in a fine, imprisonment, or both. Also, there are many jobs and financial aid programs that require Selective Service registration.

What else should I keep in mind? Registering does not automatically result in being inducted into the military.

Voter Registration

When is this relevant? When you want to vote.

What is it? Voter registration is the process of registering with election officials so you become eligible to vote.

Every state has its own voting and election rules. Depending on your state, you may be able to register online, in person, by mail, and through voter registration drives.

Why does this matter? Even if you dislike politics, voting gives you a voice in our political process. Elected officials have to consider your vision for the future because your vote matters to them.

What else should I keep in mind? You usually need to re-register to vote in a few scenarios including moving and changing your name.

Jury Duty

When is this relevant? When you are a US citizen and at least 18 years old.

What is it? Jury duty is an obligation to serve in a court proceeding as a *juror* (someone who decides if a person is guilty of wrongdoing). Potential jurors are randomly selected from various lists and are sent a *summons* (a notice to report to a court).

Being summoned does not guarantee that you will serve on a jury.

Why does this matter? It is mandatory to report to jury duty, and participating in the process may disrupt your work or personal life.

What else should I keep in mind? It is possible to postpone jury duty.

General Stuff

Appropriate Documentation

When is this relevant? When you need to prove that something took place.

What is it? Appropriate documentation is anything that clearly shows that you did what you were supposed to do, or that someone agreed to do something for you. Appropriate documentation includes receipts, income tax returns, insurance documents, contracts, and pricing quotes.

Why does this matter? Unless you can prove that something took place, it didn't. You must have appropriate documentation in order to avoid disputes over the facts.

What else should I keep in mind? Only sign documents that you understand and agree with. Purge supporting documents slowly.

Safeguarding Personal Information

When is this relevant? Anytime you are handling sensitive information.

What is it? Safeguarding personal information means sharing sensitive personal details only when absolutely necessary, and using precautions to prevent others from accessing them on their own.

Information that should not be shared carelessly includes your Social Security number, driver's license number, complete date of birth, your mother's maiden name, account numbers, account balances, and passwords.

Why does this matter? Identity theft and fraud are serious problems that can happen in the physical world or online. If you make it easy for criminals to access your information, you run the risk of becoming a victim.

What else should I keep in mind? Only give personal information over the phone if you initiate the call. Don't click on links or attachments included in unexpected emails or texts.

Setting Goals

When is this relevant? Anytime you want to accomplish something.

What is it? Goal setting is the process of identifying something that you want to accomplish and creating a plan to do it.

Goals should have the following characteristics to make them easier to achieve.

- A deadline.
- A detailed desired outcome.
- Alignment with what you want to achieve in your life as a whole.
- Consecutive stages that help you check your progress.

Why does this matter? Having goals can give you focus and purpose, and attaining them can provide you with motivation and self-confidence.

What else should I keep in mind? Start with small goals and build over time.

College Stuff

College Wage Premium

When is this relevant? When you get a job.

What is it? The college wage premium describes the fact that college graduates tend to have higher wages and better employment prospects than people with only a high school diploma.

STEM majors (Science, Technology, Engineering, and Mathematics) offer the greatest income potential.

Why does this matter? Earning more than the average worker makes it easier to afford the things you need to live, and can also help you be better prepared for retirement.

What else should I keep in mind? College is an investment like any other, so it must pay for itself as soon as possible. Degrees from low cost colleges and universities can often lead to the same jobs as expensive ones. If college is not for you, you will still need to learn a skill to make a living.

Free Application for Federal Student Aid

When is this relevant? When you need to pay for college.

What is it? The Free Application for Federal Student Aid (FAFSA) is the form used to determine how much federal financial aid you can get to pay for school.

Why does this matter? College can be expensive. Filling out the FAFSA may help you find ways to decrease your out of pocket costs.

What else should I keep in mind? Many states and colleges use FAFSA data to determine their own financial aid awards. Student aid can include grants, scholarships, work-study jobs, and loans.

Job Stuff

Resume

When is this relevant? When you look for a job.

What is it? A resume (sometimes spelled résumé) is a document that summarizes your educational background, training, professional experience, qualifications and accomplishments. It is meant to get prospective employers interested in hiring you.

Why does this matter? There are usually many job seekers who are competing for the same position you want. A resume is not only a minimum requirement when looking for a job, but it must set you apart from everyone else.

What else should I keep in mind? Resumes are often called CV (curriculum vitae).

Proof of Identity

When is this relevant? Anytime you need to verify who you are.

What is it? Proof of identity is usually a government issued document that validates that you are who you say you are. A driver's license, a state issued ID, and a passport are commonly accepted proofs of identity. Other documents that can help confirm your identity include a birth certificate and a Social Security card.

Why does this matter? Many activities depend on your ability to verify who you are. Opening a bank account, getting a job, and traveling by plane are examples of situations that require proof of identity.

What else should I keep in mind? Some organizations may also require proof that you live at a certain address. A rental agreement, mortgage bill, and home utility bill can help confirm your residence.

At-Will Employment

When is this relevant? When you have a job.

What is it? At-will employment means that your employer can dismiss you at any time and for any reason, as long as the reason is not illegal.

It also means that you are able to leave a job at any time and for any reason.

Why does this matter? Most jobs in the US are at-will, so you will rarely have guaranteed employment. However, as an at-will employee you'll have a lot of freedom to pursue new opportunities as you see fit.

What else should I keep in mind? There are many scenarios where it is considered illegal to fire an at-will employee. It is customary for employees to give 2-weeks' notice before departing from a job.

Taxes

When is this relevant? Usually when you make or spend money.

What is it? Taxes refer to money that people must contribute to the government. You will normally pay taxes for money you make, for stuff you buy, and for property you own.

The government uses taxes to fund public services and to pay for its obligations. The best known tax organization is the Internal Revenue Service (IRS), which is in charge of collecting federal taxes. However, states also have their own tax organizations.

Why does this matter? Taxes affect how much of your income you keep, and the cost of buying or owning stuff. You must file an annual **tax return** (a form used to calculate how much income tax you should pay).

What else should I keep in mind? Tax returns must be filed by April 15th unless the government officially extends the deadline. If too much money is withheld from your paycheck for taxes, you should get a tax refund. If not enough money is withheld, you'll need to pay the correct amount.

W-2

When is this relevant? When you are an employee.

What is it? Form W-2 (Wage and Tax Statement) is a document used by employers to report how much they paid you during the prior year. The form also shows the amount of federal, state and other taxes withheld from your paycheck.

Employers are required to send you and the IRS a copy of your W-2.

Why does this matter? The information on your W-2 will be very important when you prepare your tax return.

What else should I keep in mind? Independent contractors are given a different tax form.

Social Security

When is this relevant? From your first job until you retire.

What is it? Social Security is a federal program that provides monthly payments to people who reach a certain age, or who are otherwise eligible. It is funded by mandatory contributions from workers. Your Social Security number (SSN) is used to track your lifetime earnings, which determines the amount of your Social Security benefits.

Why does this matter? Social Security is only designed to cover a portion of your living expenses. You'll need other sources of income when you retire.

You'll need your SSN to get a job, collect Social Security benefits, file taxes, apply for credit, open a bank account, and in many other scenarios.

What else should I keep in mind? You can view your earnings history and estimated future benefits online.

Non-Compete Agreement

When is this relevant? When you leave your job.

What is it? A non-compete agreement is a contract that prohibits you from working for a competitor or starting a competing business for a period of time after leaving an employer.

Companies use non-compete agreements to stop ex-employees from taking their clients.

Why does this matter? Employers may fire you, or choose to not hire you, if you don't sign a non-compete agreement. If you do sign, you may not be able to work in your industry for some time after your current job ends.

What else should I keep in mind? Non-compete agreements that are overly broad or too restrictive may be less enforceable.

Non-Disclosure Agreement

When is this relevant? When you discuss sensitive information.

What is it? A non-disclosure agreement (NDA) is a contract where you agree to not share private or confidential information.

NDA's are generally used by companies to protect trade secrets, proprietary information, and confidential business details. New employees, and sometimes job interviewees, can be asked to sign a non-disclosure agreement.

Why does this matter? NDA's can force you to be silent about various matters, including some that you may find unacceptable. It is important for you to understand what you are being asked to sign.

What else should I keep in mind? Violating an NDA can have serious consequences.

Unemployment Insurance

When is this relevant? When you lose your job.

What is it? The unemployment insurance program provides payments to workers who become unemployed through no fault of their own, and who meet certain eligibility requirements.

Each state administers their own unemployment insurance program.

Why does this matter? Losing your job can put you in a difficult financial situation. Unemployment insurance payments can provide temporary relief while you start a new job.

What else should I keep in mind? If you quit a job without a good cause, you may not qualify for unemployment benefits. The system is mainly funded by taxes paid by employers on behalf of their employees.

Pocketbook Stuff

Paying Yourself First

When is this relevant? When you want to save.

What is it? Paying yourself first means that you automatically deposit a percentage of your paycheck into a savings or investment account before doing anything else with your money.

Why does this matter? Most people pay their bills first and only save if there is money left. The problem with that approach is that most of us will constantly increase our spending to match increases in income. The result is a lifestyle where there is never any money left to save.

By paying yourself first, you "hide" money in an account you don't touch. The approach works well for building your savings, emergency, and retirement accounts.

What else should I keep in mind? By setting aside a percentage of your income instead of a set amount, your savings grows with your earnings. Start small and increase your savings percentage periodically.

FDIC and NCUA

When is this relevant? When you deposit money in a bank or credit union.

What is it? The Federal Deposit Insurance Corporation (FDIC) is an agency that insures deposits in case of bank failures. FDIC insurance covers deposit accounts like checking, savings, and certificates of deposit up to a limit.

The National Credit Union Administration (NCUA) serves the same purpose as the FDIC, but it insures deposits for *credit unions* (financial institutions similar to banks, which are owned by the same people who use their services).

Why does this matter? If your bank or credit union fails, you won't lose the money in deposit accounts up to the FDIC or NCUA limit.

What else should I keep in mind? Not all banks and credit unions are federally insured. Investments like mutual funds, stocks, and bonds are not insured.

Interest

When is this relevant? When you borrow, deposit, or invest money.

What is it? Interest is simply a fee. You pay it when you borrow money, and you earn it when you save and invest it. It is calculated as a percentage, and it can be simple or compounded.

Simple interest is normally used on loans and is a fixed percentage of the original amount borrowed. Compound interest is used on credit cards, savings accounts, and many investments. Instead of a fixed amount, you are charged or paid a percentage of your total balance (including any previously accumulated interest). The ***compounding frequency*** (how often interest is applied to your balance) can be from daily to annually.

Why does this matter? If your savings or investments pay compound interest, your balance will grow exponentially because you are paid interest on the interest already earned. If your debt charges compound interest, your balance will also grow exponentially until paid off.

What else should I keep in mind? Credit cards normally compound their interest charges daily.

Savings Account

When is this relevant? When you want to save money.

What is it? A savings account is an account where you store money while earning interest.

Why does this matter? Savings accounts are useful to accumulate money for emergencies, major purchases, vacations, and annual expenses. Your deposits are normally federally insured up to a limit.

Savings accounts are less effective than checking accounts for handling day-to-day spending because they have more limitations on withdrawals.

What else should I keep in mind? Credit unions and online banks tend to pay higher interest for savings accounts. Losing a card with access to your account, or noticing unauthorized transactions, should be reported immediately to your bank or credit union.

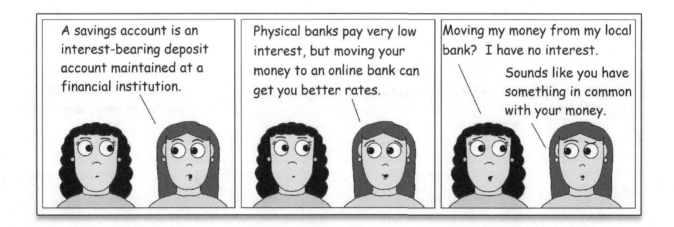

Checking Account

When is this relevant? When you need money for day-to-day spending.

What is it? A checking account is an account that gives you easy access to money you keep at a financial institution. It is normally used to pay for daily expenses like putting gas in the car, buying groceries, and paying bills.

Checking accounts usually don't pay interest, and maintaining a minimum account balance is normally required to avoid certain fees.

Why does this matter? Having a checking account greatly improves your ability to manage your finances as an adult. Your deposits are normally federally insured up to a limit.

What else should I keep in mind? Losing a card with access to your account, or noticing unauthorized transactions, should be reported immediately to your bank or credit union.

Certificate of Deposit

When is this relevant? When you are saving money.

What is it? A certificate of deposit (CD) is a type of savings account where you keep a specific amount for a fixed period of time in exchange for earning higher interest. The term can be from a few months to several years. The longer the timeframe, the higher the interest.

Withdrawing money from a CD before the agreed term normally carries a financial penalty.

Why does this matter? Regular savings accounts don't pay much in interest, so your cash grows slowly. If you have savings that will not be needed for a while, a CD can earn you more money without really changing what you are already doing.

What else should I keep in mind? CD's are typically federally insured up to a limit. Online banks and credit unions tend to offer the best interest rates for CD's.

Direct Deposit

When is this relevant? When you receive a payment.

What is it? Direct deposit describes the electronic deposit of funds into your bank account instead of through a physical check.

Why does this matter? Many employers offer direct deposit, so you don't have to deposit your paycheck in person. Since the money is transferred electronically, the funds are usually available without a waiting period.

Direct deposit can be a powerful tool to build your savings. Employers will generally agree to split your deposit between two accounts, so you can automatically divert some money to a savings account.

What else should I keep in mind? Many banks will not charge a monthly maintenance fee on your checking account if you have direct deposit.

Personal Budget

When is this relevant? When you have expenses.

What is it? A personal budget is a document that tracks how much money you are making and how much you are spending.

Why does this matter? A budget can help you manage your current expenses and plan for future ones. The lack of a budget, or the discipline to follow it, can lead to unnecessary debt.

Effective budgets prioritize savings and retirement, and clearly show where the rest of your money is going.

What else should I keep in mind? Use a calendar to help you track your paydays and when each bill is due. Budgets should include expenses that happen once a year.

Emergency Fund

When is this relevant? When you have a financial mishap.

What is it? An emergency fund is an amount normally kept in a savings account to cover unexpected financial situations.

The money is meant for things like car repairs, medical bills, losing your job, and replacing home appliances. There should be enough in your fund to cover at least 3 months' worth of expenses.

Why does this matter? Adults are expected to pay for their expenses regardless of their circumstances. An emergency fund can give you a safety net to handle financial surprises.

What else should I keep in mind? Tax refunds, overtime pay, bonuses, birthday money and other unexpected income can help build your emergency fund. Be clear about what constitutes an emergency.

Unexpected Fees

When is this relevant? Anytime you are paying for something.

What is it? Unexpected fees are charges that can be easily overlooked, or that may not be commonly known. Examples of unexpected fees are:

- *Convenience Fee* – Charged by some companies to allow you to pay with a credit card.
- *Resort fees* – A hotel charge for giving you access to specific amenities.
- *Restocking fee* – Charged when you return an item for a refund.
- *Cancellation fee* – Charged when you cancel a purchase or reservation.
- *Ticket service fee* – Charged when buying tickets for events.

Why does this matter? If your finances are tight, unexpected fees can derail your budget. You may also find yourself in a difficult position if you don't have money to pay the extra fees.

What else should I keep in mind? Always carry extra cash, or a card with access to your accounts, to pay for unexpected expenses.

Debt Stuff

Credit Reports

When is this relevant? In many scenarios involving money.

What is it? A credit report is a detailed record of how you have managed and repaid debt. It lists identifying information, account history, requests for a copy of your report, and public records.

There are three national credit agencies (also known as bureaus), which compile information from lenders and other sources to create their own versions of a credit report.

Why does this matter? Many creditors and lenders use your credit reports to determine if they'll let you borrow money.

What else should I keep in mind? The information on credit reports is commonly used to calculate a credit score. You are allowed to dispute inaccuracies that appear on your credit report.

Credit Scores

When is this relevant? In many scenarios involving money.

What is it? A credit score is a three digit number that rates your potential for paying your debts as agreed. A high score is good and a low score is bad.

The data used to calculate your score normally comes from your credit reports and includes details like your payment history and your current debts. Scores offer creditors a faster and more convenient way to make lending decisions than reviewing your entire credit report.

Why does this matter? Your credit score will determine how much you can borrow and under what terms. People with low credit scores normally get smaller loans and have to pay higher interest rates because they are more likely to not pay as agreed.

What else should I keep in mind? Potential landlords and employers can use your score to make decisions about you.

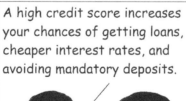

Secured Debt

When is this relevant? When you want to borrow money and you own something of value.

What is it? Secured debt is money you can borrow after providing ***collateral*** (something of value to be taken if you don't pay). Secured loans tend to have lower interest rates, longer repayment periods, and larger amounts than unsecured ones.

A ***mortgage*** (a loan to buy a house) or a loan to buy a new car are examples of secured debt.

Why does this matter? Offering collateral may help you borrow money if you don't have a credit history or your credit is damaged.

Not all secured loans have favorable terms. For example, car title loans (where the collateral is a car you own free and clear), usually have very high interest rates and must be repaid quickly.

What else should I keep in mind? Lenders can require you to purchase insurance to protect your collateral against damage or loss.

Unsecured Debt

When is this relevant? When you want to borrow money only with your signature.

What is it? Unsecured debt is money you borrow without pledging anything of value to guarantee repayment. Most personal loans and credit cards are examples of unsecured debt.

Since creditors take on more risk with unsecured debt, such loans tend to have higher interest rates, shorter repayment periods, and smaller amounts than secured loans.

Why does this matter? It is likely that you'll need to borrow money at some point, and it's better to do it without tying up your property. A good credit history can give you access to unsecured debt.

What else should I keep in mind? Creditors can still collect unsecured debt if you *default* (fail to pay as agreed).

Credit Cards

When is this relevant? When you want to pay for stuff with borrowed money.

What is it? A credit card is an account, normally accessible with a physical card, which allows you to borrow repeatedly up to a dollar limit (called ***revolving debt***).

You can either pay the full balance at the end of each billing cycle or you can carry it over from one month to the next. If you don't pay off the debt, a minimum payment will be calculated based on your balance and you will be charged high compound interest.

Why does this matter? Combining painless access to a lot of money, inexperience, and high compounding interest can easily lead to overwhelming debt.

What else should I keep in mind? Minimum payments are only designed to keep the account in good standing, not to help you pay off the balance faster.

Cosigner

When is this relevant? When you are asked for financial help.

What is it? A cosigner is a person who adds their name to someone else's loan because they can't qualify for it on their own.

Why does this matter? Cosigners are responsible for the entire loan if the primary borrower can't make the payments. Also, any missed payments generally appear on the cosigner's credit report and can affect their credit score.

What else should I keep in mind? Your cosigned debt may affect your own ability to borrow money.

Payday Loans

When is this relevant? When you want to borrow money and have no other alternatives.

What is it? A payday loan is a short-term loan for a small amount, which is normally due within a couple of weeks. The loans are unsecured and charge interest rates that are very high.

Why does this matter? Most people who get a payday loan fail to pay it on time, so they have to roll it over into a larger loan with new fees. The cycle becomes almost impossible to escape because people need new payday loans just to cover the fees of the existing payday loans.

What else should I keep in mind? Carefully look at your options before considering a payday loan.

Debt Payment Approaches

When is this relevant? When you want to pay off debt faster.

What is it? Debt payment approaches are ways to prioritize your payments to get rid of debt faster. Some people suggests listing your debts based on their interest rate, and paying them off from highest to lowest. Others suggest listing debts based on their balances, and paying them off from smallest to largest.

For either approach, the key is to make the minimum payment allowed on all debts except the one you are trying to pay off first. As you work through the list, add the payments from debt that is now paid-off to the payments you are still making until the whole list is gone.

Why does this matter? Sometimes debt cannot be avoided. You'll need to have an efficient and effective way to pay what you owe.

What else should I keep in mind? Be patient. It is normally much easier to get into debt than to get out of it.

Debt Consolidation Loans

When is this relevant? When you have several debts.

What is it? A debt consolidation loan combines multiple debts into one loan that ideally has a low interest rate.

Why does this matter? Instead of making payments on multiple high-interest debts, like credit cards, you can pay off the same total debt with less money per month. Also, making only one monthly payment will make it easier to manage your finances.

What else should I keep in mind? Make sure that you can afford the monthly payment of the loan.

Collection Agencies

When is this relevant? When you are not repaying your debt.

What is it? A collection agency is an organization that tries to get you to pay off debt you have neglected. They typically don't get paid unless you pay, so they are highly motivated to collect any ***delinquent*** amounts (not paid as agreed).

Why does this matter? Having an account in collections has a long-term negative impact on your credit. Also, it is possible for collectors to get permission from a court to take part of your wages, or money in your bank account.

What else should I keep in mind? Debt collectors must abide by certain rules.

Bankruptcy

When is this relevant? When you are deep in debt and can't repay it.

What is it? Bankruptcy is a process that allows people who cannot pay their creditors to seek relief from some or all of their debt. It is normally considered a last resort after all other options have been exhausted.

Why does this matter? Bankruptcy can help you have your debts *discharged* (you don't have to pay them back). However, bankruptcy does not excuse you from certain financial obligations like paying back student loans and providing child support.

A bankruptcy will also appear on your credit reports for many years, and will affect your ability to get future loans.

What else should I keep in mind? There are different bankruptcy types available to consumers.

Investing Stuff

Get-Rich-Quick Schemes

When is this relevant? Anytime you want to make money.

What is it? A get-rich-quick scheme is a money-making opportunity that promises lots of cash in a short period of time. It's usually described as involving little effort and no risk.

Why does this matter? Making money requires time and effort, so people are always looking for ways to minimize either factor. Scammers know how to take advantage of this dynamic.

You can be especially vulnerable to fall for a scam when money is tight because you may be desperate to improve your situation. You can also become a victim by trying to cash-in on the latest fast-money-trend that everyone is talking about.

What else should I keep in mind? Anyone can fall victim to a scammer. There is no such thing as easy money.

Index Funds

When is this relevant? When you want to invest in the stock market.

What is it? A market index is a measurement used to track the performance of a specific group of stocks or bonds. An index fund allows you to buy the same investments included in a particular index. The Standard & Poor's 500 (better known as the S&P 500) is an example of an index, which tracks the performance of 500 large companies.

The cash invested in an index fund is spread across all the companies in the fund, which lowers your risk of losing all your money. Mutual funds work the same way, but index funds have lower fees and tend to perform better.

Why does this matter? Investing in the stock market is usually a part of saving for retirement. Index funds provide a lower risk, low involvement, alternative to picking individual stocks.

What else should I keep in mind? Investing long term lowers risk by allowing stocks time to recover after a loss.

401(k)

When is this relevant? When your employer can help you save for retirement.

What is it? A 401(k) is an employer-sponsored retirement plan. It allows you to save money taken automatically out of each paycheck before taxes are withheld. The money grows tax-free, and some employers will match your contributions up to a certain limit (that's free money).

Why does this matter? When you retire, you will be responsible for paying your bills without income from a job. The government might provide you a monthly amount, but the money may not be enough to cover your expenses.

Receiving matching contributions from your employer allows your retirement savings to grow tax-free even faster.

What else should I keep in mind? Your withdrawals are generally subject to income tax. A 401(k) is not an investment. You need to determine how your contributions should be invested.

Roth IRA

When is this relevant? When your employer cannot help you save for retirement.

What is it? A Roth IRA is a retirement account where your deposits grow tax-free, and the money can also be withdrawn tax-free in retirement. Roth IRA's must be funded with taxed income from work.

Why does this matter? When you retire, you will be responsible for paying your bills without income from a job. The government might provide you a monthly amount, but the money may not be enough to cover your expenses.

A Roth IRA can provide you with tax-free money during retirement. The longer you give your money time to grow, the better.

What else should I keep in mind? A Roth IRA is not an investment. You need to determine how your deposits should be invested.

Traditional IRA

When is this relevant? When your employer cannot help you save for retirement.

What is it? A traditional IRA is a retirement account where your deposits are typically *tax deductible* (they reduce the amount of your income that can be taxed) and grow tax-free until you withdraw them in retirement. You pay income tax on your withdrawals.

Why does this matter? When you retire, you will be responsible for paying your bills without income from a job. The government might provide you a monthly amount, but the money may not be enough to cover your expenses.

A traditional IRA offers an alternative for people who want to save for retirement while getting a tax break for their deposits now.

What else should I keep in mind? A traditional IRA is not an investment. You need to determine how your deposits should be invested.

Passive Income

When is this relevant? When you want to make money without working.

What is it? Passive income is money you earn continuously, with little effort, after an initial investment of money or time. Examples of passive income include interest from a bank account, rent from a tenant, sales of a digital product you created, and ***dividends*** (money corporations give you as a reward for owning their stock).

Why does this matter? The money you can make from a job is limited by your wage and the hours in a day. Passive income, on the other hand, provides a continuous stream of money even if you are sleep.

When you rely less on income from work, you gain the freedom to choose how you spend your time.

What else should I keep in mind? Individual streams of passive income can be small, but having multiple sources can add up to a lot.

FIRE Movement

When is this relevant? When you don't want to work into your sixties.

What is it? The Financial Independence, Retire Early (FIRE) movement advocates reaching financial independence as soon as possible. That usually means saving 30 times your annual expenses and living on roughly 4% of your investments annually.

Followers of FIRE typically become financially independent many years before the standard retirement age. Their approach combines earning more than the average worker, saving more than 40% of their income, keeping expenses low, and investing in low cost index funds.

Why does this matter? Becoming financially independent, or close to it, will give you the freedom to choose how you spend your time. You don't have to stop working altogether. Instead you can work on the things you want, when you want.

What else should I keep in mind? Having debt will derail your FIRE plans. It is never too early to start saving for retirement.

Home Stuff

Household Utilities

When is this relevant? Every time you move to a new residence.

What is it? Household utilities are services that support your living space. They include electricity, natural gas, water, sewer, Internet, cable TV, landline phone, security systems, and trash pickup.

Cities generally have only one provider available for electricity, gas, water, sewer and trash. However, more options should exist for Internet, cable TV, telephone, and security services.

Why does this matter? Depending on your living arrangements, you may need to set up and pay for some or all the utilities.

If you have bad credit or no credit at all, you may be asked for a ***deposit*** (an amount meant to cover your bill if you don't pay it on time) before services start.

What else should I keep in mind? Utility bills are typically sent monthly or every other month.

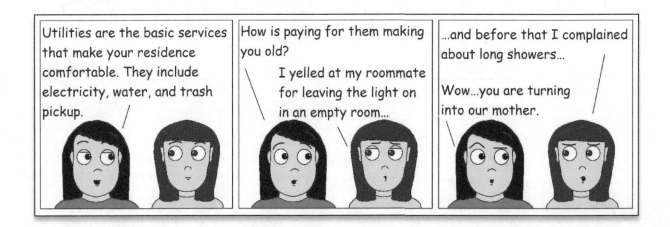

Residential Lease Agreement

When is this relevant? When you rent a place to live.

What is it? A lease agreement is a contract between a *landlord* (the owner of a residence) and a *tenant* (the person renting a residence) that allows the tenant to live in a property for an extended period of time. The agreement includes details like the monthly rent, when the lease expires, rules regarding pets and smoking, and the amount of the *security deposit* (a refundable fee generally meant to cover damage the tenant may cause to the rental unit).

Why does this matter? Since a lease locks in the rent amount and other details, it can provide more stability than renting month-to-month.

If you move before the end of your lease, you may need to keep paying rent until the lease expires or until the landlord finds a new tenant.

What else should I keep in mind? Neither the landlord nor the tenant is usually allowed to break the lease.

Renters Insurance

When is this relevant? When you want to protect your belongings while renting.

What is it? Renters insurance (some call it renter's insurance) is a type of insurance that can help you replace your belongings if they get damaged. The insurance can also cover medical and legal bills if you are responsible for someone getting hurt where you live.

Many landlords require tenants to have a renters insurance ***policy*** (a contract with an insurance company).

Why does this matter? Your landlord's insurance typically covers damage to the property being rented, but not the belongings in it.

What else should I keep in mind? Renters insurance may also pay for a hotel if the place you rent becomes uninhabitable.

Roommate Agreement

When is this relevant? When you live with roommates.

What is it? A roommate agreement is a contract signed by everyone sharing a residence to help clarify many aspects of the living arrangement.

The agreement generally covers details like the division of bills, quiet hours, household chores, overnight guests, pets, and privacy.

Why does this matter? Aside from setting rules for all roommates, the financial obligations listed in a roommate agreement can be legally binding.

What else should I keep in mind? Roommate agreements normally don't involve the landlord.

Private Mortgage Insurance

When is this relevant? When you buy a house.

What is it? Private Mortgage Insurance (PMI) is a type of insurance that homebuyers must have if their down payment is less than 20% of the home's purchase price.

The insurance is meant to protect the lender in the event you are unable to pay your mortgage.

Why does this matter? It may take you a long time to save 20% of a home's purchase price to use as a down payment. Since PMI lets you use a smaller down payment, you can keep some money for unforeseen expenses.

What else should I keep in mind? PMI is an extra payment on top of your mortgage. The insurance can be cancelled after you meet certain requirements.

Homeowners Insurance

When is this relevant? When you own your home.

What is it? Homeowners insurance (some call it homeowner's insurance) is a type of insurance that can help repair or rebuild your house if it's damaged. It may also pay to repair or replace personal items if they are damaged or stolen.

The insurance can sometimes be used to cover legal costs if you or your family members are sued for injuring someone or damaging their property.

Why does this matter? A house is usually the most expensive property people have. If you don't have insurance, you may have to pay out of pocket for a variety of mishaps involving your home, you, and your family.

What else should I keep in mind? A different type of insurance is normally needed to protect your house against damage from floods or earthquakes. Mortgage companies will require you to have homeowners insurance.

Change of Address

When is this relevant? Anytime you move.

What is it? A change of address request means that you are asking the United States Postal Service (USPS) to reroute all your mail to a specific US address.

Why does this matter? When you change your residence, you'll need to have all future mail and packages forwarded to your new home. Aside from giving the USPS your new address, you should also update it with all the people and organizations that are part of your life.

What else should I keep in mind? Mail can only be forwarded for a limited period of time.

National Do Not Call Registry

When is this relevant? When you get unwanted sales calls.

What is it? The National Do Not Call Registry is a database with a list of phone numbers that telemarketers cannot call. Certain types of calls are not covered by the registry.

Registering your phone number is free and the registration does not expire.

Why does this matter? Telemarketers can call you relentlessly to try to sell you stuff unless your number is part of the Do Not Call Registry.

What else should I keep in mind? The registry can't stop scammers from calling you.

Car Stuff

Driver's License Point System

When is this relevant? Anytime that a traffic infraction is involved.

What is it? A driver's license point system is used by many states to add points to your driver's record every time that you are convicted of a traffic violation. The number of points that is added depends on the seriousness of the infraction.

Why does this matter? Accumulating too many points within a certain timeframe will cause your license to be suspended. The points on your driver's record can also affect the cost of your car insurance.

What else should I keep in mind? You may be allowed to prevent points from going on your record by completing a traffic school course.

Bill of Sale

When is this relevant? When you buy or sell goods.

What is it? A bill of sale is a document that transfers ownership of goods from one person to another. It is commonly used to record the sale of cars, motorcycles, and watercraft.

Why does this matter? A bill of sale serves as a receipt and helps protect you against future disagreements about the transaction. It generally includes information about the buyer, the seller, and the item that was sold.

If you buy an item "as-is", it means that you accept it in its current condition and with all of its faults.

What else should I keep in mind? The sale of personal property, like animals or furniture, can also be recorded with a bill of sale.

Car Registration

When is this relevant? When you own a car.

What is it? A car registration allows a car to be legally driven on public roads. The registration on your vehicle must be renewed regularly and requires payment of certain fees.

Why does this matter? Failure to register your automobile or to renew the registration, can result in fines, penalties, and with your car being ***impounded*** (taken away until you pay the fines).

What else should I keep in mind? A car registration is different than a car title. The car title is a document that establishes the owner of a vehicle, and it doesn't need to be renewed.

Car Insurance

When is this relevant? When you drive.

What is it? Car insurance is a type of insurance that covers the cost of damages and injuries resulting from a car accident. Your insurance will usually cover people and property outside your car. However, it can also pay for damages to your own vehicle, and injuries to yourself and your passengers.

Why does this matter? Car accidents happen all the time, and the cost of addressing the fall out can be high. Insurance is meant to cover expenses that you don't want to pay on your own.

When you lease or finance a vehicle, you will be required to insure it against damage. You'll usually be responsible to pay a ***deductible*** (an amount you pay out of pocket before insurance starts to pay).

What else should I keep in mind? Younger drivers typically pay more for insurance than older ones.

Car Lease

When is this relevant? When you need a car.

What is it? A car lease is an agreement to basically rent a new car for a few years. In exchange for a low monthly payment, you can drive the vehicle up to a maximum number of miles.

When the lease ends, you must return the car in the same condition you received it minus normal wear and tear. You may also have the option to buy the car instead of returning it.

Why does this matter? When your lease is over, you don't own anything. The car will be gone and you'll be back to looking for a vehicle. Terminating a lease early, if allowed, generally costs a lot of money. High penalties also apply if you go over the miles allowed, or if the car is not in excellent shape when you return it.

What else should I keep in mind? Leased vehicles must be insured to protect the car against any damage.

Gap Insurance

When is this relevant? Anytime you finance a vehicle.

What is it? Gap insurance is a type of insurance for people who have car loans. If your vehicle is stolen or considered a ***total loss*** (the cost to repair it exceeds its value), your insurance will only pay for the vehicle's actual cash value. Gap insurance covers the difference between what the car is worth and the amount you owe on the loan.

Why does this matter? When you buy or lease a new car or truck, the vehicle starts to ***depreciate*** (lose value) as soon as you drive away from the dealer. You are responsible for the total amount of your loan, regardless of what your car is worth. Without gap insurance, the difference will come out of your pocket.

What else should I keep in mind? If someone else is at fault for totaling your car, they are only responsible for paying for the actual cash value of the vehicle.

Manufacturer's Warranty

When is this relevant? When you buy a product.

What is it? A manufacturer's warranty is an assurance that a product will meet a certain quality standard and that it will work as expected. If the product doesn't work as promised, a warranty allows you to return, replace, or repair it at no additional cost.

Warranties generally apply for a limited amount of time. They can cover specific defects or may include any type of damage.

Why does this matter? Making a major purchase can be costly. A warranty lets you know that the manufacturer stands behind their product.

What else should I keep in mind? Certain actions may void your warranty.

Extended Warranty

When is this relevant? When you buy a vehicle, major appliance, or electronics.

What is it? An extended warranty is a type of insurance that helps pay for unexpected repairs after the manufacturer's warranty expires on a product. It costs extra and may only cover specific issues.

Why does this matter? Cashiers and sales people often suggest buying extended warranties for many products.

While it is true that extended warranties can save you money when you need to repair an expensive item, they are widely viewed as not being worth the cost for most purchases.

What else should I keep in mind? Look closely at what is covered by the extended warranty.

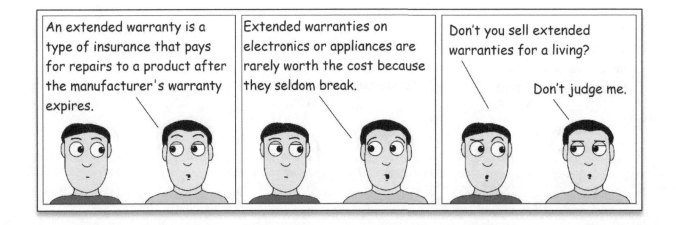

Roadside Assistance

When is this relevant? When your car breaks down.

What is it? Roadside assistance is a service that helps you handle car related problems. It covers things like changing a flat tire, towing your vehicle to a mechanic, recharging your battery, delivering gas, and unlocking your vehicle.

Why does this matter? You may not have the skills or equipment to address an unexpected issue with your car, or it may not be safe to do so. Roadside assistance is generally available 24 hours a day, 365 days a year.

What else should I keep in mind? Many plans cover you when you are driving someone else's car, and may even cover a car where you are a passenger.

Health Stuff

Health Insurance

When is this relevant? When you need medical attention.

What is it? Health insurance is a type of insurance that can pay for the cost of receiving medical care. It is normally expensive and it may not cover all medical services and procedures. Vision and dental benefits tend to cost extra.

Organizations with a certain number of employees must offer employer-sponsored health insurance.

Why does this matter? Getting injured or sick is part of life. Health insurance can help you get the care you need without wiping out your finances.

What else should I keep in mind? If your parent's insurance covers dependents, you can usually be included in their plan until you turn 26. Many plans require a ***co-pay*** (a small fee payable at every doctor visit), a deductible, or both.

COBRA

When is this relevant? When you lose your job.

What is it? The Consolidated Omnibus Budget Reconciliation Act (COBRA) is a law that allows you to temporarily keep your employer-sponsored health insurance after your job ends or a reduction in hours makes you ineligible to get insurance.

COBRA covers employees and their dependents. The insurance is expensive because your employer will no longer cover a portion of the cost.

Why does this matter? COBRA gives you a way to get health insurance while you find a new job that offers it as an employee benefit.

What else should I keep in mind? You should be eligible for COBRA even if you quit your job.

Health Insurance Exchanges

When is this relevant? When you need to shop for health insurance.

What is it? A health insurance exchange is a service that allows people to compare health plans and enroll themselves, and their families, as needed.

Why does this matter? Health insurance exchanges provide an alternative for people who cannot get health insurance through their employer or a government program.

A benefit of the exchanges is that certain people can qualify to have part of their insurance cost paid by the government.

What else should I keep in mind? Plans listed on the exchanges tend to cover treatment for pre-existing medical conditions.

Travel Stuff

Holding Your Mail

When is this relevant? When you won't be home for an extended period.

What is it? The postal service allows you to pause mail delivery to your residence during a specific time period. Similar services are offered by companies that deliver packages.

Why does this matter? It is better to have mail and packages safely stored while you are away than to have them pile up by your front door.

What else should I keep in mind? It may not be possible to prevent all packages from being delivered to your home.

Passport

When is this relevant? When you travel internationally.

What is it? A passport is an official travel document issued to the citizens of a country. It verifies your identity and nationality when you travel internationally.

Passports normally look like a small booklet that contains your photo, name, date of birth and gender. Many countries stamp your passport upon entry.

Why does this matter? You should have a valid passport to leave and re-enter the United States. Many countries allow US citizens to enter with only a passport, but some also require a **_travel visa_** (a special authorization document).

What else should I keep in mind? A passport card can be used instead of a passport booklet, but the card only allows non-air travel to certain countries near the US.

Travel Insurance

When is this relevant? When you plan expensive or international trips.

What is it? Travel insurance is a type of insurance that can help cover the cost a trip cancellation, medical emergencies, trip interruption, medical evacuation, delays, and lost luggage.

Why does this matter? You can lose the cost of your trip if you cancel prepaid or nonrefundable travel, and most US health insurance plans do not work overseas.

What else should I keep in mind? Purchasing insurance may not make sense for all trips. Insurance can help if your tour operator goes out of business.

Trusted Traveler Programs

When is this relevant? Mainly when you travel by plane.

What is it? Trusted Traveler Programs allow members to use expedited screening lanes at US airports, or when entering the US by air, land, or sea.

There are several programs to choose from.

Why does this matter? If you travel by air domestically or internationally, a Trusted Traveler Program can make the experience a little easier. The expedited process is designed to be faster and more convenient than the standard approach used at security checkpoints.

The program can make a big difference when you are running late to catch a flight, or if you have health concerns over the radiation from body scanners.

What else should I keep in mind? You can be randomly selected to go through the standard security screening.

Life Stuff

Marriage Certificate

When is this relevant? When you get married.

What is it? A marriage certificate is a document that verifies that two people are legally married.

Prior to the wedding, a marriage license must be obtained. The person officiating the ceremony will send the license to the proper government official, so the marriage can be recorded and certified. Each state has different rules about when and if marriage licenses expire, and about the required waiting period between obtaining a license and getting married.

Why does this matter? A marriage certificate is typically required if you want to change your last name to that of your spouse, change your marital status for insurance, and get benefits associated with your spouse.

What else should I keep in mind? A few states recognize common law marriages, which do not require couples to have a marriage license or a ceremony.

Safe Deposit Box

When is this relevant? When you need to store something valuable.

What is it? A safe deposit box is a secure container that is usually kept in a vault at a bank or credit union. The box is rented and is used to store things like jewelry, important documents, and collectibles.

Why does this matter? Sometimes your house may not be the best place to keep certain valuable objects or hard to replace documents.

Typically, you are the only person who knows what is in your box and the only person who can access it. To retrieve the contents of your box, you'll need to visit the branch during business hours, provide proof of identity, and have your key available.

What else should I keep in mind? Federal deposit insurance does not cover the contents of a safe deposit box.

Small Claims Court

When is this relevant? When there is a dispute over money.

What is it? Small claims court is a special court where disputes involving small amounts of money can be heard by a judge. Attorneys are normally not allowed and the cases tend to be resolved quickly and inexpensively.

Why does this matter? Small claims court may be an option when you are unable to settle a financial dispute on your own. Examples of issues that are addressed in small claims court are:

- Getting back your rental security deposit.
- Trying to collect a small debt from an acquaintance.
- Having the responsible party pay for your injuries or damaged property.
- Having a company perform the services agreed on a contract.

What else should I keep in mind? The court will not collect the money for you, but it will provide you with documents to help you do it.

Class Action Lawsuits

When is this relevant? When you are part of a group that has been harmed.

What is it? A class action lawsuit describes many individuals, who have suffered similar losses or injuries, bringing a combined case against the responsible party.

Most people learn about their eligibility to join a class action after receiving a notification. Members of a class action generally don't have to do much until the case is settled.

Individual compensation related to a case may be small.

Why does this matter? It is likely that you'll receive a class action notification at some point. You should understand it before joining the class.

What else should I keep in mind? Class actions can take years to be settled.

Life Insurance

When is this relevant? When people depend on your financial support.

What is it? Life insurance is a type of insurance that pays your ***beneficiaries*** (people you select to get your money) a lump sum in the event of your death.

"Term life" insurance is the most commonly purchased type of life insurance, and is known for its affordable ***premiums*** (monthly payments).

Why does this matter? When you pass away, you can no longer provide for people who depend on you financially. The money from your life insurance can partially or completely replace your financial support.

What else should I keep in mind? Complicated life insurance products are not necessarily better for your needs.

Last Will and Testament

When is this relevant? When you are married, have children, or have assets.

What is it? A last will and testament is a legal document that provides instructions about what to do with a person's assets after they die.

Why does this matter? If you don't have a will, a court will decide what to do with your belongings and minor children in accordance with your state's laws.

What else should I keep in mind? There are several types of assets that are automatically inherited by a surviving spouse.

About the Author

Witty Ryter is a creative guy who likes to write stories and draw cartoons. His comics have been featured in trade publications in the US and abroad.

Over the last few decades, Witty has been learning how to be a grown-up. In that time, he has done many of the things that typical adults are expected to do like graduating from college, working for money, getting married, starting a family, buying a house, paying lots of bills, trying to save and invest, and traveling a bit.

Now in middle age, Mr. Ryter wants to use his experiences to help young adults be more prepared for the challenges of being a grown-up. He has included in this book many of the basic nuggets of knowledge he has picked up along the way, and hopes that they provide some guidance to 18-year-olds who view adulthood with bewilderment.

OTHER WORK BY WITTY RYTER

Witty Ryter

MONEY QUESTIONS
TO ANSWER BEFORE 30

Simple Ways to Get Your Finances Straight

Made in United States
Cleveland, OH
18 December 2024

12126960R00057